Homesick for the North
and Other Poetry

©2021 Catherine West-McGrath

The right of Catherine West-McGrath
as the author of this work
has been asserted by her
in accordance with
the Copyright Designs and Patents Act 1988.
All rights reserved, including
the right of reproduction
in whole or part in any form.

ISBN: 9781916320079
Imprint: Independently published

Other poetry collections
from Catherine West-McGrath:

Lapsed Capitalist: A Poetry Collection

Optimistic Activist: Poetry and Verse

British Values: A Poetry Collection

What She Really Means and Other Poetry

Try This, It Might Help: Poetry & Verse

The Poems

To Hear A Poem 1
Glad That I'm Alive 2
Your Life is a Poem 3
Homesick for the North 4
Whose Story? 7
Musical Chairs 8
Have Algorithms Disadvantaged Me? 9
Amnesia Pandemic 10
Microphone Megaphone 11
Protest Song 12
Soulful Creator 13
Somethings Can Only Be Mended By Artists 14
A Proper Job? 15
Water Finds A Way 16
Your Seat Has Been Taken 17
As A Women 18
Wake Up Pretty 19
What's Wrong With This Picture 20
Radical Self Love Bombing 21
Angel in the Marble 22
Success 23
Lifeboats 24
Ideas 25
This Poison Can Be Diluted 26
When You Grown Up I Want You To Be... 27
On Rediscovering Bedtime Stories 28
Stubborn Door Part 1 29
Flying Kites 30
Sisters 31
Deaf and Dumb 32
In Therapy 33
Tree Surgeon 34
Ode to Elisabeth 35
In the Psychiatrist's Office: Psychiatrist 36
In the Psychiatrist's Office: Patient 37
Shine A Light 38
FEAR 39
Join the Dots 40
Coats 41

The Truth Will Set You Free 42
Help 43
The Overgrounders 44
Direction of Sail 45
Allies 46
Stubborn Door Part 2 47
Storyteller 48
A Week of Spring Haikus 49
On Valentine's 50
The Test 51
And His Fingers Make the Church Roof 52
The Harbour 53
You Scribbled On My Pages 54
Chance Meeting 55
Lonely Together 56
Changed Lock 57
Wall 58
Birthday 59
Bites and Stings 60
Let Our Love 61
We Are Dancing 62
Mosaic 63
Love Poem 64
An Exquisite Age 65
Earth Takes a Rest 66
And In That Slow Time 67
What Happened to the Humans? 69
Let's Leave the Past Where it Belongs 70
Healthy Relationship Mindset 71
There is a Person 72
Let My Compass Be Compassion 73
Jazz Blue 74
We Will Listen to Leonard Bernstein 75
How to Fall Asleep 76
Love Manifesto 77

The Lyrics

A Thousand Drops 78
The Same for You 79
The River 80
Things I Should Have Said 81
Separate Minds 82
A Heart Full of Love 83
Elephant 84
After the Earthquake 85
Postcards from the Fairground 86
Lineage 87
Miraculous 88
Imagine We Did It 89
The Stories We're Creating 90
Lotus Flower 91
Yellow Kite 92
Wake Up in Blue 93
The Islands are my Tomorrow 94
Girlfriends 95
Jigsaw 96
Her Daughter's Right Here 97
Conversations In Autumn 98
Put Down Your Shield 99
False Friends 100
Thrive 101
Authenticity 102

To Hear a Poem

To hear a poem is to be favoured
To write a poem paint with words
To speak a poem is to hear your voice
To read a poem thoughts are heard
To walk a poem tread most carefully
To swim a poem dive in deep
To wake a poem is to start a fresh
To dream a poem rise from sleep
To sculpt a poem is to chisel rock
To melt a poem light a flame
To build a poem is to place each brick
To birth a poem give your name
To kiss a poem is to shape a mouth
To hold a poem lift it high
To love a poem is to know its truth
To trust our poem can never lie

Glad That I'm Alive

I am not the waves which push me
I am not the current's pull
I am not the stinging hailstorm
Or the clouds which try to dull

I was born to swim in oceans
I was born to float and dive
I will find my calmer waters
And be glad that I'm alive

Your Life is a Poem

First fighting
    flesh feeling family
Hospital corridors
Breathing new life
Welcoming home
Your life is a poem

Toy teddies
    tantrums toilet training
Reading stories
Rock a bye baby
Carried in arms
Your life is a poem

Books bedtimes
    bicycles best buddies
School days
Homework
Falling out and in to friendship
Your life is a poem

Heartbreak heartache
    hoping hoping hoping
First dates
First kiss
First love
Your life is a poem

Applications apprehensions
    aptitude aspiring achieving
First pay cheque
First home
First car
Your life is a poem

Childish childlike
    childfree childful childcare
The child inside
The child teaches you
The child reaches you
Your life is a poem

Income impact
    influence interesting insightful
Making your mark
Making your money
Making a home
Your life is a poem

Respecting repairing
    relaxing relying reflecting
Taking care
Taking a break
Taking another tablet
Your life is a poem

Passing ships passing strangers
    passing time passing by passing on
Paying our dues
Paying the florist
Paying their respects
Your life is a poem

Create connect
    converse confess contest
Write about it
Shout about it
But whatever you do
    don't be afraid to live it

Your life is a poem

Homesick for the North

An invite to a Southern home
Perhaps I wouldn't feel alone
How kind of them to offer lunch
Was told they were a friendly bunch
And coats hung up and scarves unwound
Soon talk turned to my holy ground
My accent let my new friends know
I'd left the North some years ago
'But oh how grim' they had to tell
'Back streets that look like living Hell'
And once again I did defend
My land, my family and friends
'How lucky you were to move out
Your education paid no doubt
And set up home, you must have wowed
Your parents must have been so proud'
I tried to tell them all I missed
But they would just not hear of it
'Such culture here and art so rare
How barren it must be up there
And conversation must be more
Intelligent without the poor'
But I had been there many times
So reaching down in to my mind
I told them of the pride within

Homesick for the North cont.

That patch of Earth they could not dim
That grew such brave and fearless minds
To explore worlds and make new finds
Discover truths for all to know
And protests won so we could grow
Then music, literature and art
The North was there right from the start
Sons left to fight in foreign parts
And daughters left with broken hearts
New industry seduced with pay
But kept production's means away
'But why then is there such despair
And dreariness, is it the air?
I've watched the programmes on TV
A journalist went up to see
He tried to find and spoke to folk
To understand why they were broke'
'Enough of this North South divide
What we need now is common pride
Surely what's best for our fine country
Is just more of some equity'
And then a guest was keen to tell
How their properties were doing well
But talk soon turned excitedly
To Northern English history
The type I thought was really cool
Not that I learned it while in school

Homesick for the North cont.

A complex web that took its toll
On farming, cotton, steel and coal
Sometimes neglected, blamed and shamed
Often ignored, abandoned, gamed
Its children might have had to flee
To take new opportunity
Like I was then sat in my chair
Away from home yet always there
Then one kind guest who'd heard me try
Speak of my pride and tell them why
Said, 'Most sat here I bet can trace
Some ancestry back to this place
It's not then such a foreign land
But lives that we can understand'
Soon each one lifted their disguise
Declaring their own Northern ties
Sometimes through ones own family tree
Or where they'd studied their degree
And then we all agreed this space
Deserved to take its rightful place
Deserved to have its story known
Deserve to have its money shown
I stepped into the southern air
And so I did not long despair
I made a plan to catch a train
And see my Northern home again

Whose Story?

Who wants to hear my story?
Who decides what I can tell?
Does my gender or my skin tone
State if others know it well?
Whose feet are elevated?
How do they take the stage?
Whose hand can hold the mic?
Whose letters form the page?
Does power hold the high bar?
That lets one version through?
Or money say my blunt vowels
Should not be listened to?
If my legs are made of steel wheels
Or my vision is too blind
Does it mean my short novellas
Are not worthy of your mind?
Or because my mind was broken
Where I scrambled down to hold
Does it mean the words I rescued
Should be left out in the cold?
Do the rules around my grammar
Make me fear to ask you why?
Lest a mark put in the wrong place
Means I shouldn't even try
Do you seek to silence my voice
If my accent isn't clean?
So you feel justification
To ignore the words I mean
Does the length of my flowing locks
Lock me out of the debate?
Or because I hide my features
Mean no place for my portrait?
But I know one day you'll hear me
And my story will get through
My colours lit so vibrant
Then you'll have to see what's true
For my chapters will explain how
All these stories came to be
And my words will fill the white space
In your books of history
You'll want to hear my story
You'll strain to see my view
For the story of the unheard
May be your story too

Musical Chairs

The lesson today is musical chairs
There's only so many so just be aware
Sometimes there are many
But most times there's not
We like to remove to
Have fun with you lot
The aim of the game is to stay on a seat
Until we decide that it's time for a treat
Then we'll make you run round
To comply and compete
To distract from the fact of our little deceit
And even if you try to build your own seat
We may still remove it in crushing defeat
But to stop this all folly
You must work as one
And create something new
Which will see this game gone

Have Algorithms Disadvantaged Me?

It's starting to affect emotionally
Have algorithms disadvantaged me?
I think about my failed GCSE
Rejected by that university
I thought it was down to complacency
But what about a postcode lottery?
The cities left behind by industry
And towns cut down by harsh austerity
Believed the myth of meritocracy
While others benefit financially
Advantaged more so by their ancestry
Access to power remains hereditary
It's starting to affect emotionally
Have algorithms disadvantaged me?

Amnesia Pandemic

It's seven o'clock
Here are the headlines you're waking up to
A pandemic of amnesia has swept the planet
No one can remember who we are required to hate
We don't even know who to hate for starting this
Or who to blame for spreading it
A spokesperson for the government said,
'This is quite extraordinary.
Every morning our media outlets
Wake viewers and listeners with a regular reminder
Of who they are to hate and blame
In case they have forgotten overnight'
We now go to the editor of a major newspaper with a huge online presence
'This really is unprecedented
All our reporters, even myself, cannot remember
Who we are required to hate and blame
In order to serve our readers who rely on us
Every morning we remind them
Who to hate
Who to blame
So that they may get on with their productive day
So that they can keep the peace
So that they may stay compliant
So that they may keep the powerful in power'

Microphone Megaphone

Microphone Megaphone on a stage not alone
Microphone Megaphone on a stage not alone

Silenced since little child
Grew up angry vicious wild
Turned within hurting core
Painful muscles hurt no more

Microphone Megaphone on a stage not alone
Microphone Megaphone on a stage not alone

Gagged and bound in a cage
Broke the bars in a rage
Turned away from every ear
Even love that came too near

Microphone Megaphone on a stage not alone
Microphone Megaphone on a stage not alone

Drawn to story telling's might
Sees in power justice fight
Left with nothing no real choice
Silenced throat that finds its voice

Microphone Megaphone on a stage not alone
Microphone Megaphone on a stage not alone

Protest Song

I am fierce
I am strong
Ain't no place
I don't belong
I'll protest
I will fight
Till afforded
All my rights
Don't you try
To silence me
I will roar
Through history
We have played
By your rules
But you've taken
Us for fools
Well we're taking
No more
Leave your privilege
At the door
We will fight
What is wrong
We will sing
Our protest song

Soulful Creator

The soulful creator
Works at their craft
Practising, practising
More hard graft
In dark early mornings
Remembering dreams
Urging to write
Designing their scenes
Stealing a minute
To draw a new line
Imagining visions
Unearthing a mine
Over and over
Checking each trace
The clay in their hands
Created in space
For no other reason
Their message to state
Rewarding enough
And needs no high rate
Eschews golden trinkets
Their talent innate
The soulful creator
Just needs to create

Somethings Can Only Be Mended By Artists

Some things can be mended by ourselves
Some things can be mended by family
Some things can be mended by friends
Some things can be mended by neighbours
Some things can be mended by volunteers
Some things can be mended by teachers
Some things can be mended by doctors
Some things can be mended by professionals
Some things can be mended by business people
Some things can be mended by spiritual leaders
Some things can be mended by politicians

And SOME THINGS CAN ONLY BE MENDED BY ARTISTS

A Proper Job?

What job is proper?
Viable?
What job is
Justifiable?
What used to be?
But isn't now
Though it may be again
But we're unsure how

With venues quiet
And theatres dark
Now it's difficult
To make our mark
But the doors are closed
Seats stored away
While distance keeps
The crowds at bay

But for us these jobs
They aren't just pay
They're reasons to get up
And seize the day
They're a chance to connect
A chance to inspire
To be filled with the source
That fuels our desire

With jobs like these
Worth more than gold
Not just wages earned
But tales to be told
They're more than proper
They're part of us
And won't be extinguished
By a new virus

We plan and fix
We problem solve
We collaborate
And show resolve
We share our talents
Bring people together
We entertain
We just make things better

We make this life
Worth living for
We show what's human
Connect to core
We electrify
We energise
These aren't just jobs
These are our lives

But without a plan
We'll stay in the shade
The lights on dim
The sounds on fade
The laughter muted
The cheering diminished
Without a plan
Entertainment is finished

Then songs unsung
And stories untold
Sets packed away
And theatres sold
Till years from now
We'll reflect and say
'Remember the fun
We had back in the day'

Water Finds A Way

Like hydrogen and oxygen
Music and marks
Like molecules
Movement
Like hydroxil ions
Words
The water will find
A way through the rocks
We were born to create
And every barrier
To our creativity
Will be met like
Water meets a barrier
We will find every tiny route
To create
To liberate
To communicate
Adjusting its shape
Adapting to its environment
Drop drop dropping
Through the levels
We were born to create
And every barrier
To our creativity
Will be met like
Water meets a barrier

Bathing the weary
Filling the empty
Spraying the nature
Diluting the poison
Splashing the children
Cooling the heated
Refreshing the thirsty
Cleansing the dusty
We were born to create
And every barrier
To our creativity
Will be met like
Water meets a barrier
Pushed against a dam
Like an angry crowd
Waiting to burst
With crashing waves loud
Flooding the plains
Soaking the earth
Showering the people
Anointing at birth
We were born to create
And every barrier
To our creativity
Will be met like
Water meets a barrier

Your Seat Has Been Taken

Your seat has been taken
Removed by a virus
Your view's been restricted
Not that you could see us
No we were the people
Excluded by wealth
And now you can see
How it's hurting your health
You're missing the charge
The electrical buzz
Did you ever consider
What that void did to us?
You felt a connection
To humanity
Felt plugged in to life
And a community
Each story and sound
They filled up your cup
Events which brought hope
So you didn't give up
But now you can see
That your calendar's clear
How sad you can feel
When you lose things once dear
But we want to implore
When your seat's free once more
To remember those who
Never got to the door

As A Woman

As a woman I have held your hand
Tried to understand
As a woman I have aimed to please
Learned of my disease
As a woman I have held my tongue
Believed I was wrong
As a woman I have tried too much
Calmed you with my touch
As a woman I have put you first
So you don't feel worse
As a woman I've been told my place
Shown my pretty face
As a woman denied rights to books
Praised the way she cooks
As a woman my reproductive state
Has determined fate
As a woman I've been pushed to try
Sometimes to get by
As a woman I've had lesser pay
But that's not okay so I'm going to say
Every message played
Through each brief decade has my story made
Now I question all
Straight and standing tall
Scaling every wall
I see what you've tried
Truth was that you lied
Blamed the tears I cried
As a woman I am human too
Human just like you
Now see what I'll do

Wake Up Pretty

Wake Up Pretty
Spring Fashion You'll Envy
Lose inches in weeks
My best friend betrayed me
Have great sex tonight
Date a millionaire
Could this pill make you thin?
Ways to wear your beach hair
Avoid wardrobe disasters
Find swim wear that flatters
How to please him in bed
Her reputation in tatters
How to wear a white shirt
Botox secrets revealed
Celebs in their new homes
Cook these wonderful meals
Make your bathroom a spa
This year's favourite look
Tips to beat facial hair
Read it in her new book
Power through menopause
Lush new makeup to wow
Try these cool summer shades
Learn the power of now
Joy of tidying up
Cut your clutter today
Keep your thighs in great shape
Check out this holiday

Breathe

Breathe

And we wonder why we
Feel we're not good enough
When bombarded by this
Which attacks our self love
There's no rule here to say
We must do what they say
See them differently
No need just to obey
Question what they create
Try to fuel our desire
Keep us busy and poor
Turn us into a buyer
We don't have to comply
We can choose not to read
Leave them there on the shelf
Leave their profits to bleed
Choose to use our own mind
Not an editor's view
I'm just perfect as me
You're just perfect as you

What's Wrong With This Picture?

Tell me about the olden days
What was it like back then?
And is it true that women were perceived
As less than men?

Did newspapers still show us
Like dolls dressed up to play?
And chose to see the things we wore
Not hear what we could say?

Did advertisers make us buy
Their masks so we would feel?
More confident to show ourselves
And hide that which was real?

Did women reading us the news
Have to be dressed to shine?
But men who told us of events
Could pass along just fine?

I'm glad that things have changed since then
That people saw its lies
So women now are heard and seen
Not just in their disguise

Radical Self Love Bombing

Radical
Self
Love
Bombing

Sometimes it's the only way
To turn a new page in our book
Turn night into our day

Radical
Self
Love
Bombing

Exceptionally kind
Accept those faults that we all have
And leave our shame behind

Radical
Self
Love
Bombing

Be proud to be just you
Accept the darkness and the shade
Of all that you've been through

Radical
Self
Love
Bombing

You're someone else's light
They look to you for hope and joy
Your vision is their sight

Radical
Self
Love
Bombing

Sometimes it's all we need
And when we leave our cage of fear
That's when we know we're freed

Angel in the Marble

The angel in the marble
Waits buried deep inside
Formed deep beneath the cold stone
No longer needs to hide

The angel in the marble
Will soon be touching air
Will bring the world its beauty
Will see its truth laid bare

Success

The dictionary definition of 'Success' is 'the achievement of results wanted and hoped for'
So...
If you're accepting yourself just as you are:
You're successful to me.
If you're forgiving yourself for any mistakes:
You're successful to me.
If you're being as kind to yourself as you would be to a good friend:
You're successful to me.
Because that's all I've ever wanted and hoped for you

Lifeboats

I'll teach you about your boat
So that you may sail it on the water
In rough seas and in calm seas

I'll teach you to mend your sails
To notice the small tears
So that they may be fixed before ripping in two

I'll teach you about the keel
The piece underneath
To keep you upright and in balance

I'll teach you about building a lifeboat
Or two or three
So that if your boat tips you will at least have one life boat

And if others boats tip
I hope you can offer them a lifeboat
Without expecting anything in return

And if you should ever lose all your boats
I hope others will remember your kindness
And offer you refuge

Ideas

Ideas have shaped our history
And our society
Ideas tell us what to expect
What you can take from me
Ideas that spread through media
Come rushing down the line
Until we think ideas as fact
Have been here all the time
But all they are or can now be
Are just someone's idea
They might work till they just don't work
Or till we see more clear
So question whose ideas you choose
To live your one life by
Don't blindly choose another's thoughts
In case they're just a lie

This Poison Can Be Diluted

All around me
Thick thick
Poisonous liquid
Stings with its sharp taste
Poured in to my glass
From flickering tubes
On radio waves
And staining ink
Always trying to pull us apart

But I have water in my bones
Welling up from springs
Formed millions of years ago
Whose atoms are magnets
For human connection
Although now dispersed
And with every breath
And thought
And word
This poison can be diluted

When You Grown Up I Want You To Be..

Joyful Inquisitive Confident Proud
Courageous Playful Inspiring Loud
Respectful Listener Speaker Aware
Fulfilled Creative Curious Fair
Hopeful Resilient Powerful Leader
Confident Vulnerable Open Reader
Compassionate Loving Thoughtful Respected
Amused Intelligent Assured Connected
Questioning Challenging Disruptive Wild
But most of all Happy
For you are my child

On Rediscovering Bedtime Stories

'Can we have a bedtime story?'
I delight at your request
Knowing that these evenings
Are the ones I love the best

I search upon the bookshelf
For one to suit this night
I pause among the chapter books
To find the one just right

We read the books by candlelight
Take turns to read the pages
Make voices for the characters
Connect despite our ages

Agree we'll make a habit
Of making bedtime reads
And afterwards we hug goodnight
My heart has all it needs

Stubborn Door Part 1

Faced door laughing back
Never open me
Still being a reasonable and level headed sort of person
And after careful consideration
Took keys attached to belt
Selected one most comfortable
Worn warm key form fitted fingers knew so well
Used almost everyday for other stubborn doors
Nothing
No reassuring click sigh of release
Hard resistance
Therefore being a reasonable and level headed sort of person
And after careful consideration
Poked prodded stabbed jabbed that one familiar hot key
Whispered under breath
Threw favourite key attached to
Unfamiliar Untested Unheard
Acquaintances to floor
Yet being a reasonable and level headed sort of person
And after careful consideration
Pulled door's hand banged fists on chest
Kicked foot against legs
Until holes left by hands and feet in clothes
However being a reasonable and level headed sort of person
And after careful consideration
Took five steps backwards
And with deep intake
Ran right shoulder first towards door
Tripped over bunch thrown down

Flying Kites

Make a suggestion
Fly a kite
See which message
Catches a light
Try out a thought
See how it lands
Consider the critics
Who won't understand
Pull at the strings
See where it goes
Imagine it falling
Crashing too low
Seek social proofing
Supporters behind
What message is needed
To influence minds?
Which stakeholders need
To get all on board?
Who must give their backing?
What can you afford?
And just as you think
It's all good to say
The kite disappears
Job done for today

Sisters

Oh my sisters and the worlds that we created
Are much bigger than we ever could have known
Touching people who will read our tiny word books
Rolling out from this our hill top country home

We are daughters mourning for our Cornish mother
Who has left us when she died so very young
But we're cared for by our Irish curate father
Who'll outlive us in a life that will last long

And the stories and the poems that we weave here
Of the lives that live with love despite their fears
Will touch hearts of people we won't ever know yet
To be read by generations down the years

Deaf and Dumb

You don't know that you're dumbstruck and silent
You don't wait for a noise to come out
Why listen for drumbeats of anger?
When you don't even know you can shout

Years staring at weed choked cracked pavements
You've forgotten to lift up your head
Lulled by echoes that constantly told you
Just to keep yourself watered and fed

Because nobody bothered to listen
Your voice flew away like a bird
But I know that your heart holds a whisper
And a story that longs to be heard

In Therapy

I spoke to the therapist
And she was so kind
I looked at her quizzically
'Can't you see in my mind?'

'Did you mishear me?
Not get what I meant?'
'Your feelings are valid'
Yet more compliments

'But all of my life
I've hated this force
Repelling attraction
Felt magnetic force'

'Entirely normal
Not unusual at all
In fact it's quite healthy
These things you recall'

'You mean that I'm human
Have been all along?'
'I'm quite certain of it
You did nothing wrong'

Tree Surgeon

I once felled a trauma
It dropped deep in me
And sank to the bottom
Like the trunk of a tree

It remained still and quiet
Then a storm came to town
Where a boulder dislodged
Which had held it fixed down

But the trauma took chances
It rose to the top
I clung on to the trunk
Hoped the storm would soon stop

Should I wait for the calm?
Let the trunk sink again
Or lift from my lake
Would it be worth the pain?

But I met a tree surgeon
Who believed that I could
So the trunk became shavings
Which we threw in the woods

Ode to Elisabeth

What is the lesson here?
What is the stage?
There must be a reason
To feel all this rage

Didn't Elisabeth
Teach me of grief
Is that why it hurts
Now I've lost my belief?

I'm trying to bargain
To negotiate
To right an injustice
To lessen your hate

But tired of my pleading
I know I need rest
I sink to the bottom
Defeated at best

But after depression
I know there will be
A time of acceptance
My soul will feel free

I know I'm not dying
I've chosen to live
And in my new life
I'll choose to forgive

I've climbed up the stages
My heart feeling mended
Remembering Elisabeth
And the dying she tended

In the Psychiatrist's Office: Psychiatrist

Well you're just a mix of chemistry
With electric in there too
If I take or add some chemicals
All will be alright with you
I won't ask you any questions
Because memories are not real
Though I love to love my memories
Love the way they make me feel
But if you can see bad memories
Then you mustn't let me know
Just take your medication
And the pain is sure to go
What's the point of listening to you
You're upset too much to speak
Though I see you talk to others
That we label here as weak
I'll confront you with your weakness
Only fair to show what's wrong
I won't show you any kindness
No point letting you be strong

In the Psychiatrist's Office: Patient

You ask me how my mood is
As if I'm meant to know
When knowing what feels happy
Has left me long ago
Like asking how's my English
Not checking how I spell
Or accepting my first answer
When I've learnt to lie so well
And to understand my own mood
I would need a sense of me
But I'm buried in self hatred
And you pile on more daily
I've lost friends you once confronted
They'd lost hope and you could see
That your casual assessments
Might hang them eventually
Take my tablets all my life now
So I'll keep you in your pay
I'd prefer us to be equal
So we both might thrive one day

Shine a Light

Shine a light in those dark places
Open up the heavy door
Take a step out of the shadow
Lift the cloak bring to the fore

Not defined by being somewhere
Where you didn't want to be
You detached so couldn't feel
Closed your eyes so couldn't see

Turn your picture round and show it
Let it be a tale of strength
Now a page that was once buried
Can be read in full at length

Take the hand of one you left there
Leave them hidden deep no more
And together you can show
The beauty still within your core

FEAR

FEAR - is a message heard to think a different way
FEAR - is a chance to think 'What if it's all okay?'

FEAR - is a telescope that seeks a different view
FEAR - is a microscope to offer up a clue

FEAR - is a question we may have answered wrong
FEAR - is a narrative we've listened to so long

FEAR - is a whispering that 'maybe it's not so'
FEAR - is a lightning bolt to force us to let go

FEAR - is a shaking ground to help us find our feet
FEAR - is a friendship new that's waiting just to meet

FEAR - is a chance to grow to change our story's plot
FEAR - tells us we're alive in case we have forgot

FEAR - is a hidden door to open to be brave
FEAR - is a golden prize within a darkened cave

FEAR - is the first small step out of a sunken hole
FEAR - is the light that tries to reach our buried soul

Join the Dots

Join the dots
Stay curious
See the white space
Between
Notice patterns
Hold the page close
Take steps away
Trace the path
Number the marks
Which ones
Followed which
Appreciate the shape
Cover parts
Uncover parts
Where are strokes missing?
What is being hidden?
Who told you that wasn't necessary?
Why did you listen?
Join the dots

Coats

On sunny days I wear a coat
To keep my arms in shade
On rainy days I wear a coat
To keep the drops away
On snowy days I wear a coat
To keep me feeling warm
On stormy days I wear a coat
To keep me safe from harm

But once I wore a heavy coat
Its lining holding stones
So even when I was embraced
Those rocks would press my bones
I thought the coat belonged to me
As though it were my skin
Forgotten it was just a coat
Just covering within

Regardless of the coat I wear
That's all that it can be
A coat I choose to wear or not
That coat is never me
And so is it how I behave
And how at times I feel
These do not form the core of me
Instead the coat I feel

The Truth Will Set You Free

You say 'The truth will set you free'
And I feel heard so beautifully
I learn to trust so I can speak
My voice once silence starts so weak
But slowly thinking you'll be kind
Remembering tears you've left behind
Knowing how much I wanted healing
Now surprised by what I'm feeling
Encouraging to seek out cures
To learn that which our soul endures
To shine some light on shaded heart
Hopeful sadness may depart
I feel the time to tell my side
To no more sense the need to hide
You say 'The truth will set you free'
And I reply 'Do you mean me?'
You say 'The truth will set you free'
And I enthuse so willingly
I listen while you speak of shame
We laugh at this pathetic game
Encouraged that you'll lend an ear
Or why else would you be so near?
While others told me to ignore
Injustice which had gone before
Or silenced me dismissed my thought
Or ended days with fights hard fought
I saw in you a kindred friend
To understand and not pretend
To show compassion in my pain
To know the hold of trauma's stain
You say 'The truth will set you free'
And I reply 'Do you mean me?'

Help

Help doesn't have to be advice or medication
Help can be 'I'll sit with you to ease your situation'
Help doesn't have to be a place of isolation
Help can be a hand to hold a hug or conversation

Help doesn't have to be clinically assessed
Help can be 'I'll share with you a time I faced a test'
Help doesn't have to be 'You're not coping well'
Help can be 'I also have a similar tale to tell'

Help doesn't have to be 'I know what's wrong with you'
Help can be 'I understand because I'm human too'

The Overgrounders

The Overgrounders are the ones who live above the ground
They might have always lived there or recently have found
Their feet are light and move with such delight and joy and grace
To savour precious moments in their happy peaceful place

Unlike the Undergrounders who stay stuck down below
Their eyes fixed in the dark preferring not to know
Their feet and legs are bounded by bandages of fear
Still wading through the darkness in waterways of tears

The Overgrounders like to feel the sun upon their face
They see the beauty all around and joy fills up their space
The Undergrounders sometimes hear faint noises from above
But quickly will dismiss the sounds as echoes of self love

The Undergrounders oft were told, 'It's safer neath the soil'
So keep their heads fixed downwards and moan about their toil
Sometimes an Undergrounder will climb towards the light
Leaving their safe discomfort to see the stars at night

And when they do they still can be surprised by what they see
A festival of wonderment and curiosity
Yet even Overgrounders might stumble to the floor
But rather than sink underground they learn to rise once more

Direction of Sail

If you believe you are sailing
In to a dark storm
Every set back will seem
As part of the permanent storm
And your focus will be
On sailing
In to that darker storm ahead

If you believe you are sailing
In to a sunny day
Every set back will seem
As a temporary rain shower
And your focus will be
On sailing
In to that sunny day

Allies

I am your ally
Your partner in healing
I'll listen not judge
Let you feel what you're feeling
Want you to thrive
Not stay in the past
And always stay patient
However it lasts
Know that your future
Is waiting and bright
Not offer opinion
What I think is right
Trust that your spirit
Knows its direction
Will find the right path
Without my correction
And if you should stumble
Or find some steps tough
I'm here to remind you
You're always enough

Despite what we're told
We're not here to compete
Just find our true selves
Those parts to complete
Uncover some truths
Past hurts hurting still
Accept that the process
Can test any will
And when you have taken
Some small steps ahead
Perhaps you'll help me
Sort out my own head
Then you'll be my ally
My partner in healing
And listen not judge
Let me feel what I'm feeling

Stubborn Door Part 2

Landed twisted broken against cold tiles
Groaning expletives
Door standing above
Keys fingers stabbing
Piercing chest
Painfully lifted
Freeing bunch from weight
Reunited with favourite key
Denied
Unfamiliar
Untested
Unheard
Acquaintances on floor
Still being a reasonable and level headed sort of person
And after careful consideration
Came to sensible conclusion

Sleep on it

Try same key again tomorrow
Warm key form fitted fingers knew so well
Used almost everyday for other stubborn doors

Storyteller

You are a storyteller
Your words make people feel
You mix the angel's cocktail
To make them think they're healed

And by your story telling
Is how you got to steal
But now we know you know we know
Your stories are not real

You are a storyteller
You love to feel our eyes
Your stories bring attention
For all you sacrificed

You are a travelling rover
Move quick don't get too close
Ensure you're always leaving
The ones who loved you most

A Week of Spring Haikus

Opening shed door
Find Spring bulbs have awoken
Life grown in cold womb

                              World turned upside down
                              But more beautiful because
                              We see more clearly

Winter may decay
But dying leaves give birth to
Yellow daffodils

                              Through the old window
                              Dried blooms waved a March goodbye
                              To fresher cousins

Tiny Spring garden
Brings delight on April walk
Burnt trees fragrance air

                              See how deep purple
                              Is enhanced by bright yellow
                              No coincidence

Tulips by doorstep
Is the daffodil a weed
Refugee or guest?

On Valentine's

On Valentine's I went to church
On a busy Dublin street
To find remains of a Roman saint
I thought I ought to meet
His few remains were locked inside
That small reliquary
I felt his spirit yearn to leave
No more a prisoner be
I kissed the chest that with him in
Had reached the Irish shore
And I imagined you right there
So thought of you some more
On leaving I felt winter sun
Faint blue broke through the cloud
I found myself in Temple Bar
Among its younger crowd
Each one of you had visited
The Dublin streets had tread
Either to live or passing through
This then your common thread
Some conversations I recall
I listened then more than
But sure we walked its many streets
No long term love your plan
And each new meeting pushed me on
To find who I should be
Till in that Dublin street I knew
My one true love was me
Retracing steps I did return
Went back to find the place
A pilgrimage to Valentine
His holy, sacred space
To tell him I had learnt my task
Compassion was our key
And with that key I turned the lock
To set the poor saint free

The Test

Two old men in a sunlit room
Concerned about the boy
There's something wrong but what to do?
Perhaps he needs a toy
We need to see of what he's made
To see him at his best
A girl will challenge him I'm sure
Then let one be his test
So there he found her in a field
Within the landscape view
And after his soft kiss to her
He warned 'I will hurt you'
Then later on within that room
Invited in for tea
She sat under their watchful gaze
Looked awkward silently
And when she left they smiled inside
They knew they'd chosen well
She will not speak of this we think
She'll never want to tell
And so they judged he'd passed the test
They let him have his prize
But what he'd seen was burned in him
Could never leave his eyes

And his Fingers Make the Church Roof

How did we get here?
An oldish man with white hair
Sits with his back in an armchair
A dark room with books and untidy tapes
Tea and biscuits on a tray
I sit eager to please
Awkward feeling my arms are too long
You stand equidistant

We
are a
triangle

He smiles and pours me tea
You make a joke and we laugh nervously
He joins his hands and his fingers make the church roof
He asks questions and nods
I search your eyes for assistance
You're even further in the distance

Why did you bring me here
To this house with too many rooms?

The Harbour

At this moment in time
I am standing looking across the water

It is empty now
But I know one day
A boat will come along
To carry me over to
The other side of my life

I hope that the crossing
Will be as beautiful as the time spent
In this harbour
With you

And I shall never forget
The gentleness of your love
And my liberation from loneliness

You Scribbled On My Pages

I know you found and scribbled on my pages
And doodled arrows straight across my heart
But your graffiti won't erase my spirit
A whole person cannot be torn apart

I felt you try to push me under water
You didn't know how strong that I could swim
I felt you try to break where I was fragile
With no idea that's where my strength begins

I know you used your weight to make me lie down
I know you liked to see me on the ground
But I learned moves to simply flip you over
And I can spin and turn myself around

I know you found and scribbled on my pages
You thought my words would never see the day
You mocked the marks I made within my notebooks
But I knew I had something real to say

You tried to take my pen and then my keyboard
You said that those like me should not be heard
But times have changed and more of us are speaking
So sorry if it leaves you so disturbed

Chance Meeting

When I am sixty
And you are seventy
We will have a chance meeting

We'll tell each other how happy we are
We'll remember the time we thought
We were the loves of each other's lives
We'll joke that we had a lucky escape
How it all would have been an awful mistake

We'll stop at a tea shop
And tell each other how the years have passed

I'll be the first to leave
As I close the door I'll pull my scarf up high
Blaming the wind for the sting in my eyes

Lonely Together

We shared a space yet miles apart
We tried to verbalise our heart

And reaching in to an oft hid place
Hoped words would find each others grace

But our backs turned those angry eyes
Communicated our despise

We tried to find a common ground
Still silence was the loudest sound

We couldn't see the soul in front
Let anger rage and fear confront

Two people lost inside a home
Together yes but still alone

Changed Lock

Well rested
We had spent that morning talking
You left to make an errand
And we had hugged

I wrote a thank you note
Then left it on the table
For you to find on your return
Just in appreciation

I closed the door behind me
To take a walk cheerfully
But on my return I found the key
Would not turn in the lock

I banged on the door
But only heard silence
Then you passed me a note through the letterbox
'It will be some time...'

Wall

I was a wall
For you to project
A black and white wall
For you to neglect
Or cover your image
Who you thought I should be
So I learned to be shamed
Of the pictures of me
All the pictures I'd chosen
Were judged not quite right
So I took down the frames
And I turned off the light
Soon my wall turned to ice
I could no longer feel
If I stayed in the dark
Your projections weren't real
But I once felt a sunbeam
I remembered its heat
I stretched out my hand
And I felt my heart beat

I repainted my wall
With bright sunny hues
Drawing vistas and scenes
With inspiring views
Penning lyrics and music
Adding fabrics to hold
Soon my wall was a stage
Where my stories were told
I constructed some shelves
Which I filled with my words
And I sent out my voice
On the wings of wild birds
Now I see with my eyes
And my soul starts to sing
There's no reason to hide
From this beautiful thing
So there's no longer room
For your image to fall
No room for your shade
On my colourful wall

Birthday

All of a sudden
Your birthday became
Just another day
In the calendar
Not celebrating you

In fact I didn't notice
The date at all
Except that it was
Just another day to
Celebrate me

Bites and Stings

We're we both cursed by some Faustian pact?
To gain all this life meaning each must retract?
To wallow in grief to feel so bereaved?
To realise nothing is what we believed?

We're we the players in some devil's game
With rules to stay silent or end up in shame?
Did some passing stranger place on us a curse?
When we were just infants so life would get worse?

Or must we still wait to find out the truth?
To be reunited with love from our youth?
We're we ever a story or just a mistake?
Do we ever regret the choices we make?

Should we be so dramatic must it all be a play?
Should we just realise things can turn out this way?
Should we give them a chance those who wait in the wings?
While we hope they don't find all our bites and our stings

Let Our Love

Let our love be a journey
And not a destination
Let our love grow daily
Not wither in stagnation

Let it open like a flower
Slow invisible
So we hardly even notice
We are indivisible

Let our love slowly show
Let it take us by surprise
Let it be in a smile
Or the way we use our eyes

Let it be a caring word
And an effort to be kind
So we slowly realise
We have made a precious find

We are Dancing

We are dancing

Masculine and Feminine

Yin and Yang

Giver and Receiver

Two sides of one coin

Pushing and pulling

Balancing

To create a beautiful

Equilibrium

We are lifting and lifted

Fire and Water

Earth and Sky

Mosaic

I am a fine mosaic life
Made up of broken parts
Each piece created carefully
A stunning piece of art

I shine with colour light and shade
My diamonds catch the sun
Each piece makes up the whole of me
I cherish every one

Each sharpened edge gained painfully
Each grouted corner healed
And in that mess of broken tiles
My beauty is revealed

Love Poem

You're my safe space
You're my happy place
I see in your face
Beauty, love and grace

You're my now and here
You're my all that's dear
Kindest voice to hear
You're my free from fear

You're the sun's warm rays
You're my special days
When it's all a haze
You're my favourite gaze

You're your shoulders broad
You're a hug adored
You're my love outpoured
Where my heart is stored

You're a soothing balm
When I sense alarm
You're a sea of calm
Refuge from all harm

You're my deepest stare
You're my depth of care
Want my life to share
You're my everywhere

You're your smiling eyes
You're your laugh surprise
When you hear my cries
You're my paradise

You're a soft warm bed
You're my cradled head
And my favourite med
Is all that you've said

You're my brightest light
You're my sweetest night
When it's all alright
You're in line of sight

You're my favourite drink
You're my cheeks go pink
At the kitchen sink
You're my nice to think

You're my sacred sound
You're my deep profound
Where my heart is found
You're my homeward bound

You're my hand to hold
You're my shield from cold
When I'm very old
You're my story told

An Exquisite Age

An exquisite age is when you finally understand
You are the one you've been searching for
You are your better half
You are the one that will complete you
You are the message story and song you need to hear
You have a treasure within you
You are not your emotions
You are your best friend
You are accepted just as you are
You are a masterpiece and a work in progress
You have talents which may be deeply hidden
You are missed when you're not around
You are enough
Your voice deserves to be heard
You can learn a lesson
You can make mistakes
You can change your mind
You can turn around
You can take a new path
You are the sun and the moon and the stars
Your blood and bones contain the cosmos
You hold galaxies in your teardrops
You are a way for the universe to know itself
Your DNA looks like magnificent stained glass
You are at one with nature
You hold all knowledge inside of you
You are exquisite

Earth Takes a Rest

Please slow down
I need a rest
Your constant growth
Too much a test
Stop in your tracks
Take in the view
Change habits ways
Restore renew
Rethink your plans
Please turn around
Remember I am sacred ground
Reflect how quick
We are infected
Reminds us how we're all connected
My one system a fine balance
Restore it while we have a chance
We've changed in an emergency
Let's carry on for you and me

And in that Slow Time

We learned to live quite differently
We learned how to slow down our pace
We stopped to admire the view
The beauty surrounding our space
We noticed our neighbours anew
When sat in their garden or step
We nodded a 'how do you do'
Some new that we'd never yet met
We noticed the things on our street
Things hurriedly rushed by before
We looked at things curiously
Were thankful for food, nature's store
We took care to structure our day
Made ceremonies last longer too
Like using a pot for our tea
Or letting the coffee beans brew
We shared recipes with our friends
And learned how to bake bread and cake
We learned we had talents and skills
And felt good for what we could make

And in that Slow Time cont.

We mended and sewed broken clothes
We found at last things to repair
We started to grow things from seed
And tended those seedlings with care
We took dusty books from the shelves
And read classic novels at dawn
We learned to recite childhood rhymes
And novels and screenplays were born
We framed photos sat in our drawers
And painted fresh scenes with a brush
Or captured a view for a print
So careful we didn't need rush
We played games with children at home
Or camped in the garden at night
We chatted with friends on the phone
Our letters began to hand write
We saw those who care in new light
The nurses and drivers in blue
We sent thanks into the night sky
And in that slow time we all grew

What Happened to the Humans?

Humans who inhabited the female form were oppressed by humans who inhabited the male form

Humans whose skin was black were oppressed by humans whose skin was white

Humans born on one part of the planet were oppressed by humans born on another part of the planet

Humans without money and possessions were oppressed by humans with money and possessions

And humans who were vulnerable because of illness or age were oppressed by humans who were powerful because of health or age

Their intelligence was very highly developed but intelligence wasn't enough to save them

Unfortunately, they were very deficient in compassion both for themselves and for other humans

They never learned that unless everyone was encouraged to thrive no one could thrive

They never learned that humanity could only survive when no human was oppressed

So they didn't survive

Let's Leave the Past Where it Belongs

Let's leave the past where it belongs
We've learned so much since then
Let's not give up this chance we have
To start, begin again
To keep connected to our home
Our neighbours and our Earth
To tread much gentler than before
To witness nature's birth
Let's forge a future new and bright
Let's all respect our health
And build a kinder future world
Where connection is wealth
Let's lift each other when we fall
Let's love the Earth we share
And treat resources that we use
As precious, unique, rare
Let's understand connectedness
That kindness can be caught
Let's not waste all we've learned this time
Let not it be for nought

Healthy Relationship Mindset

And in the end
I realised
I just
Wasn't
Interested
In finding
Someone

Instead
I was
Interested
In finding
My own
Healthy Relationship Mindset

And
Possibly
Someone
With a
Healthy Relationship Mindset
Too

There is a Person

I'm told there is a person
Who is coming down the hill
At the gate they'll stop to meet me
And we'll take the path until

When our fingers touch like soft breath
As we cross the rushing streams
Never running out of kindness
We will share each others dreams

I've been looking out the window
And I've heard some feet pass by
But their boots have been too heavy
So I doubt that they could try

I'll know you when I see you
Your eyes will let me know
You've been told there is a person
And you've willed to make it so

Let My Compass Be Compassion

Let my compass be compassion
When I'm faced with words of hate
Whether to me or another
Let compassion be the gate
So that when I meet a sorrow
That might seep into my core
Let that gate prevent its entry
So that peace will be my store

Let my compass be compassion
Let me choose a higher grace
So I do not take a wrong path
Leading to a darker place
Where I focus on forgiveness
And acceptance of my state
And in doing so a kinder and
More loving world create

Jazz Blue

The jazz player's tune
Transports me
Standing in starlight
Washes over me

I am on a balcony
Looking on a city street
Figures below
Above a bakery

I am a singer
In a smokey club
Now at the table
Now the microphone

I am the saxophone
At one with the pianist
Freestyling
Carried away

                    I am in a hot street
                Running through a sprinkler
                      Throwing ice
                      Sitting on steps

                      I am thinking of
        George Ella Billie Miles Nina Amy
                    Gregory Kamasi
                      I am thankful

                    I am nine years old
                Holding Rhapsody in Blue
                      Could music
                    Ever last so long?

We Will Listen to Leonard Bernstein

We will listen to Leonard Bernstein
And read Auden's poetry
We will quote Virginia Woolf
And have guests come round for tea
We will sit among the cut flowers
To elevate our minds
Discussing latest ideas and rare artistic finds
We will gather in our salons
To while away our day
Whilst reading some Jack Kerouac
Or Ernest Hemingway

How to Fall Asleep

I enter the room to see only friendly faces
Welcomed I settle in the space around me
Brought fragrant tea
Cool breeze a river flows one window to the other
Outside trees move leaves gently brushing
Sweet smelling flower garlands cross ceiling
Treasured books half remembered lines stocked on tables
Join in
Favourite artists projected on walls
Join in
Each take turns to talk listen soothe
Respectfully with compassion
What do we talk of?
Over remains of music?
About our day and the pains of past days
Anything troubling us is considered carefully
The solution is always to
Forgive myself
Forgive herself
Forgive themselves
Tomorrow is another day
Pulling a soft blanket over shoulders
Eyelids heavy
Sense breath slowing
Head swirls in sounds smells sensations
Until breathing in and out
In and out
In and out
In and out
In
And
And in the morning
I leave them to their conversations

Love Manifesto

It's not the who but what we'll be
It's not the look or game
It's what we'll bring not what we'll take
Not who we'll choose to blame

It's not the one, twin flame, soul mate
We'll not believe their lies
It's our intention to create
That will define our ties

We'll understand we need to work
To understand our own
Our reasons why we make a choice
Not curse the other one

We'll leave at times so we can seek
Adventures we can share
To return back with tales and truths
We'll find our passions there

We'll not expect something we won't
Expect within ourselves
We'll look inside to be aware
Like seeking books on shelves

We won't expect each to complete
An emptiness we feel
Our completeness is ours to find
Not others we can steal

We'll make the time to nurture care
So each one will be heard
We'll not neglect our precious love
Our tiny fleeting bird

We'll take an interest in the goals
The ones which fuel our drive
And love the passion that we know
Gives meaning to our lives

We'll show compassion every day
We'll make sure we are kind
Communicating what we can
The stories in our mind

We'll be two equal spirits whole
We'll complement the other
We'll create space to fuel desire
Attentive but not smother

We'll let each live their life
To learn and stretch and grow
And thank each other for the gift
The love we've come to know

We'll learn to trust
We'll make it so
And sign our Love
Man - if - esto

A Thousand Drops

I felt another drop of kindness
Fall on my gate today
Leaving behind the bread and apples
Asking 'Are you okay?'

And who knows what we leave behind us?
A thousand drops of love and kindness
And who knows what we'll leave behind today?

You travelled over a thousand miles
To be there at his side
To watch him as he fell asleep
And afterwards we cried

I felt another drop of kindness
Fall in my hands today
Leaving behind a children's rainbow
Asking 'Are you okay?'

        You travelled over a thousand doorsteps
        To let me know you cared
        I heard applause fill up the sky
        On evenings that we shared

        I felt another drop of kindness
        Fall on my eyes today
        Leaving behind a wave through windows
        Asking 'Are you okay?'

        You travelled over a thousand notes
        To let us share your stage
        To play some music for my soul
        Tell stories from your page

        I felt another drop of kindness
        Fall in my heart today
        Leaving behind a hopeful future
        Asking 'Are you okay?'

The Same for You

Could you really love me?
Once I saw it on a screen
I mean worship and adore me
Are you hearing what I mean?

It's the push and pull
Of loving some how
It's the dream I hope comes true
Like a king and queen
In a movie scene
And I'll do the same for you

You can't see my stories
Hidden bruises in my heart
Where instead of growing closer
Well I've only grown apart

Saw two lovers walking
Taking care to sooth and tend
And I'm sure I heard them laughing
Like they had their own best friend

Will you listen if I murmur?
Hold my hand if I reach out?
Treat me kindly when I falter?
Will you let me have the doubt?

Things I Should Have Said

After the storm is over after the hurricane
I'm gonna run through debris be near you again
After the rain's done falling after the flooding stops
I'm gonna climb up ladders run across roof tops

Things I should have said
But fear got in the way
Thought I had more time
But look at me today
My life's slipping away

After the fire stops burning after the flames are out
I'm gonna walk on hot coals leave you in no doubt
After this pain is over after my body heals
I'm gonna dance on stages show what my heart feels

After my tongue is mended after my voice returns
I'm gonna shout from towers tell how my heart burns
After my heart stops breaking after the pieces mend
I'm gonna fly by mountains stay until the end

Things I should have said
Things I should have said oh
Things I should have said
Things I should have said oh
Things I should have said
Things I should have said oh
Things I should have said
Things I should have said oh

Things I should have said
But fear got in the way
Thought I had more time
But look at me today
Things I should have said
But fear got in the way
Thought I had more time
But look at me today
My life's slipping away

The River

Have you ever stood in a dry river bed?
And the stones hurt your feet?
And the dust hurt your head
I was dying of thirst I was frightened to try
But I needed the water without it I'd die
(Without it I'd die)

I need the river
(The river to wash over me)
I need the river
To carry me into the sea
(Into the sea)

Yes I built that dam was a long time ago
But that body of water
Had nowhere to flow
And I made you both lean keeping that wall upright
Where I'd asked you to stand at a distance just right
(A distance just right)

If we're made of water then we're made of love
Like the stars in our hearts
Are the stars from above
And I heard that great river it screamed to be free
So I knocked down the wall and I swam to the sea
(I swam to the sea)

Separate Minds

Don't talk to me about emotion
I would rather swim the ocean
Than listen to what you feel inside
Don't let me know just how you're feeling
I would rather spend the evening
Just touching souls but in separate minds

A physical attraction chemical reaction
I know you felt too
But it burns out like a star
Emotional connection drifting to affection
Is what it's gonna take
If we're gonna go that far

I felt a little crush but I didn't wanna rush
In case I got it wrong
And I would be a fool
You caught me of my guard I was falling pretty hard
I know its all too late
And I broke my golden rule

I'm asking if you care but I see your never there
And even if you were
You'd be another place
And wishing it was so won't make it real I know
I just have to accept
I'm too easy to replace

A Heart Full of Love

So when you spoke to me
I didn't hear your voice
I only heard his angry tones
And when you held me close
I didn't feel your warmth
I only felt him in my bones

I'm sorry I thought I heard you say
You're too much you'll never be enough
If only I'd put that girl away
And heard you say
My heart is full of love

And when you looked at me
I felt a predator
Was out to capture me like prey
So when you reached for me
I felt the pull of time
I ended up at yesterday

And then you held me close
And I was in your arms
And I knew that this was where I'd stay
We took a taxi ride
I could at last confide
That things were different in that day

Elephant

The elephant tied to the rope
Grows up and cannot see
That it is stronger than it thinks
So stays close to the tree

Oh elephant
With your sad sad eyes
I hope one day
That you realise
The circus just relies on you to feel
You're weaker than you are
But it's not real
No it's not real

You're not back in those ancient days
It's different now you'll see
What's keeping you afraid to pull
Your rope from your own tree

So break the bars that keep you in your cage
And break the fourth wall of your home made stage
The latch can't keep you locked in anymore
And the street awaits beneath your own trap door

The circus trainer has to hope
You'll never realise
You have the strength to be released
And set free from their ties

After the Earthquake

Walking through the house today
Sunlight hits the wall
Broken bits of broken brick
The room becomes a hall
And gifts and souvenirs I had
Now sharp and torn
The dust that covers everything
I am reborn
(Now I am reborn)

After the earthquake
I'm still here
But I leave behind
An empty house
Where we played sometimes
But I've somewhere new to find
(New to find)

Still in clothes from yesterday
Plaster in my hair
Stepping carefully throughout
Trying not to care
I grab a notebook and my voice
I need to leave this place
I wonder how can people disappear
And vanish without trace
(Without a trace)

Grab some photographs I had
Address book with your name
Think that's all I'm going to need
It's gone and it's a shame
Step in the sunlight
The ground solid once more
The earthquake made my house fall down
But left an open door
(Left an open door)

Postcards from the Fairground

You found me underground
And curled up in a ball
A frightened bird with beating heart
I hadn't felt the sun
Forgot that I could run
But then you changed me from the start

I never knew that there was a fairground here
I never knew what there could be
I only saw the shadow in my shade
Until you gave your arm to me
I grabbed on tight to you I started my ascent
But when I stepped onto the ground
As I turned round to show you what I saw
You were nowhere to be found

I wrote you everyday
I wished that you were here
I sent you pictures of the merry go round
I heard the music play
I think I heard our song
I hoped you might just hear the sound

I wish that you could see
Just what you did for me
I wish you'd see me now I fly
I hope all's well with you
I wish your dreams came true
I wish you hadn't said goodbye

Lineage

Our lines entwined
We were doing fine
And we held memory
Their blood our veins
Just to start again
It was our territory

You and I
We had our stories
Then our worlds collide
We see the dark
That cloaked our lineage
And we brought the light

A bowl inside
For the hurt to reside
But we don't pass it on
That story ends
And we make amends
A new one has begun

No longer links
In a chain that sinks
We can break the mould
Our secrets out
They can never doubt
Because our story's told

Miraculous

On this mote of dust
Suspended in a sunbeam
On this pale blue dot
We learned to call our home
You unlocked a puzzle deep
Within my being
So no longer do I need
To feel alone

You took me on a magic carpet ride
You told me of the stars I had inside
You taught me about how we're all connected
The energy from you to me
Expands my curiosity

You told me I was a phenomenon
You gave me hope when all my hope was gone
You let me see this wonderous world anew
The energy from you to me
Creates our new reality

You said I'm a miraculous machine
Of atoms organised in this great scheme
Your voice can set the fireworks in my mind
The energy from you to me
Released my soul and set me free

Imagine We Did It

Imagine imagine the dolphins
Imagine imagine the bees
Imagine imagine the forest
Imagine now covered with trees
Imagine the petals imagine the leaves
Imagine they're breathing
When our crowded world flees

Imagine imagine the starlight
Imagine imagine the night
Imagine imagine the moon there
Imagine when dark skies are bright
Imagine the ocean imagine it's clear
When turtles can swim there
And they've nothing to fear

Imagine our daughters imagine our sons
Imagine they're playing enjoying the sun
Imagine they're laughing imagine they say
Our imagination made a difference that day

Imagine imagine we did it
Imagine imagine we would
Imagine imagine our joy if
Imagine we knew that we could
Imagine our habits imagine our dreams
Made all of this real
Do you know what this means?

The Stories We're Creating

Oh the stories the stories we're creating
The stories we're creating in our mind
About those we love and those we hope to find

So what if I grabbed the fragments of the truth?
No hurried explanation no excuse
I found what I was looking for because
I didn't want to see for what is was

So what if I thought you'd be there at the end?
And every call meant you were my best friend
I put a filtered rainbow up to you
And a technicoloured world became my view

So what if I heard was not your truth at all?
What if the good was all I could recall
Denying you might ever do me wrong
I had a choice but still I played along

Lotus Flower

To unfold out of dirt and mud
To feel the life within your blood
To rise up high is in your power
The beauty of your lotus flower

And you you are a lotus flower
Oh you your beauty is to know
In you that everything else that happened
To you has power to help you grow
(Has power to help you grow)

In yearning only to be known
Your petals are now felt and shown
Delighting those and all who see
Your wonderous precious purity

Awakening anew each morn
You love to feel the sun reborn
And there's a hope in every hour
Because we know the lotus flower

And you you are just meant to rise
Oh you you're meant to feel the sun
On you in all of the darkest places
Of you your growing was begun
(Your growing was begun)

Yellow Kite

When she was at your door
She asked for nothing more
'What are you here for?'
That's when she needed you
And crying through her pain
She hung her head in shame
Had nothing more to gain
That's when she needed you

And now she's standing by the sea
A yellow kite held in her hand
It's so delicious to be free
Things turned out better than she planned

And up her yellow kite taken
Into a sunny azure sky
Seems sad to let her heart be broken
Won't let the summer pass her by

When you made her heart leak
When you refused to speak
Made her think she was weak
That's when she needed you
When you were feeling sad
She you gave all she had
'I'm sorry that's too bad'
That's when she needed you

Wake Up In Blue

A new love you feel it too?
A new love I see in you

I can almost see the atoms dancing
(Catching the light)
I can almost hear them as they're crackling
(There in plain sight)
I think you see them too
There's a string of stars from me to you

A new friend I'd love to know
A new friend where will we go?

I wasn't listening but I heard your voice
The stars were pulling me I had no choice
I woke to see the sunlight on your face
The universe conspired for us to share this place

A new page our story reads
A new page but where it leads?

A new sky wake up in blue
A new sky I'll give to you

The Islands Are My Tomorrow

I see the islands up ahead I'm safely out of the bay
I'm patching up my boat again I know I'll be okay
The cove was fine for a little while but it ain't no place to stay
The islands are my tomorrow the cove was my yesterday

I was sailing my boat in the water
When I noticed the rain clouds ahead
But I didn't expect in the morning
That my sails would be torn into shreds
I was foolish I thought I could handle
Some dark clouds that had threatened my view
But I guess that the sailor inside me
Had a lesson to learn maybe two

Well I lit up the sky with my signal
And out came a boat to my sight
When it towed me back into the harbour
And that's when the storm reached its height
There were others who needed some shelter
In that cove by the rocks where we fell
And we cared and we tended each other
We had magical stories to tell

Other boats that came up along side me
With their sailors so patient and kind
But I know that their own boats were battered
By the storm raging on in their minds
I unfolded my map of the islands
I was hopeful by what I would find
What I didn't require for my journey
I was happy to leave far behind

Girlfriends

It's so good to see you
And tell what I've been through
You wouldn't believe the year I've had
And how are things with you?
And how's the family doing?
What are they up to now?
After the storms were brewing
Will it be calm from now?

Girlfriends you hold my dreams with care
Girlfriends I know you're always there
Girlfriends who could have known back then?
Girlfriends we'd still remember when

The lovers come and move us
The children steal our hearts
The plans we thought would build us
Sometimes tore us apart
But you stayed true through all times
With just the same calm smiles
Our dreams took us new places
But we can stay a while now

You were so kind to me
When I forgot I could
Advising gen-tle-ly
But never said I should
Reminding me of joy
My spirit soured so high
I never laughed so long so loud
I am so proud to call you

Jigsaw

I am broken and I am tired
I am worn out and I've been hired
I'm distracted by the news
And all the pretty pills I get to choose

Child learns to find a door a door beneath the stair
Finds a cave to find some shelter find some shelter there
Hiding is the only game they know
Breathe relief the footsteps as they go

Then the mother leaves a box a box outside the door
Jigsaw with the picture gone the picture gone for sure
Pieces pieced together make a heart
Better when together than apart

Soon the child can hear the boots the boots on stairs above
Remembers this is not the sound not the sound of love
Dragged out from their hiding place is found
All the pieces falling to the ground

Mother you'll see the passion deep within my soul
He tried to conquer but he never will control
And when I'm all grown up I'll learn to use my strongest power
And pick those jigsaw pieces up within your darkest hour

Her Daughter's Right Here

She loved her nature she touched the land
She knew her body she'd seen the plans
She saw the universe in a tear
And felt the seasons of the year

She saw the healing in the flower
She talked to trees and knew their power
She bled in rhythm to the moon
And played a wild and haunting tune

Going down down in the water
Down down in the water
Someone's sister someone's daughter
Going down in the water
Gonna burn burn in the fire
Burn burn in the fire
Hear her scream as the flames grow higher
Gonna burn in the fire

She nursed the mother and baby born
She wrapped the bodies when time to mourn
Well she's a witch and a bitch and a whore in their view
And her daughter's right here singing back at you

Conversations in Autumn

Sometime is a long long time away
And sometimes it feels only like yesterday
And sometimes I'm walking down a path
Kicking up the falling leaves and never looking back

I never asked you didn't say
I much preferred the quieter way
You always carried it so well
Some things it's better not to tell
Can't we just stay and watch the fall
The changing meaning of it all
It's only just becoming clear
Things fall apart this time each year
And conversations in autumn
Conversations in autumn always start this way
And conversations in autumn
Conversations in autumn always start this way

Sometimes I'm feeling all at sea
Sometimes I remember how you rescued me
Sometimes my ship is only going down
But I'm playing with the band and hanging on for one last sound

Sometimes I am just the trees
Standing with my fallen leaves in all my vulnerability
Sometimes I'm standing in the rain
Knowing it's the only thing to do if I'm ever gonna blossom again

And conversations in autumn
Conversations always start this way
And conversations in autumn
Conversations in autumn always end this way

Put Down Your Shield

I used an umbrella to
Protect me from the rain
But I forgot to put it down
When it was dry again

I used a shield of cold steel
When arrows flew to me
But when the fight was over
My shield stayed so heavy

And my soul was still weeping
It cried please set me free
All these things you think will help
They just imprison me

I covered cuts with bandage
I left it there to heal
But when the wounds had grown new skin
I knew not how to feel

I built walls to protect me
Not knowing in my pride
The walls would only serve to harm
And hurt my soul inside

I felt my soul was dying
It needed light and air
I left my shield and shelter then
To let it know I care

These things I know I don't need
At least not everyday
Sometimes it's best if we are brave
To throw them all away

False Friends

I'm trying to remember how we first met
You'd think it would be so hard to forget
We've known each other for so long we four
But now it's time I showed you out my door

And as for shame
I tried to play your game
I tried to please your judging eyes
But now I realise we'll never be the same
And dearest fear you always stayed too near
You made me want to run away
But when I chose to stay your lies became too clear
And then you hate the one who showed up late
You offered poison like a wine I saw it just in time
You nearly were my fate

You clung to other people that I knew
And other wounded souls believed in you
You told them you were right but they were wrong
You sold your dangerous spells your poisoned songs

You found me hiding in my weakest place
Disguised as just another friendly face
Well now the game is up my three false friends
I think our long acquaintance has to end

Thrive

Do you want to crawl through rose gardens
And only eat the thorns?
Do you want to scratch your skin on stones
But stay off the lush green lawns?
Do you want to be stung by angry bees
But not take taste the nectar sweet?
Do you want to wear someone's heavy boots
Not feel grass beneath your feet?
Or do you want to love yourself
So much you're glad to be alive?
Do you want to thrive?

Do you want to take your punishment
Because that's what's good for you?
Do you want to live in fear
Of every nightmare coming true?
Do you want to wear an armour
That's too heavy just to crawl?
Do you want to hear their laughter
When you take another fall?
Or do you want to love yourself
So much you're glad to be alive?
Do you want to thrive?

I'm gonna get up to the top of the mountain
I've turned my back on the valley of fear
I'm gonna get up to the top of the mountain
I can almost see the valley from here

Do you want to go into the cave
And find your treasure chest?
Do you want to see who you could be
If only you could rest?
Do you want to own your story
Say you've finally passed the test?
Do you want to show compassion
To the child who tried their best?
And do you want to love yourself
So much you're glad to be alive?
Do you want to thrive?

Authenticity

Authenticity
Comes creeping up on me
Taps me on my shoulder
And wakes me from my dreams
Authenticity
Says time to follow me
Connecting me to heart and soul
And what my spirit needs

I can't promise you that I will make it easy
Or everybody wants to hear what you will say
But I'll promise you that you will fall in love again
With that young child you locked behind your heart before today

Take the boy who knows the name he has been given
Isn't right for him he wants to choose for her
Or the girl who loves another girl but someone
Feels too angry and says that it's not right for her to care

Take the woman who couldn't speak of past wrongs
Finally finds a voice for things she has to say
Or the man who needs to take a new direction
Knowing that path would only lead him further in harms way

www.ingramcontent.com/pod-product-compliance
Lightning Source LLC
Chambersburg PA
CBHW021156080526
44588CB00008B/364